The Rejoice of Celestial Odyssey

Starlit Pathways: "Voyage to the Infinite"

ROHAN . S

Dedication

I dedicate this journey to my family, teachers, friends and neighbors whose unwavering support and belief have been the guiding light through every challenge. May we all continue to reach for the cosmos, embracing the mysteries and wonders that await us beyond the horizon. For the dreamers who gaze at the night sky, yearning for adventure among the stars. To those whose boundless curiosity ignites our quest for knowledge and exploration.

Acknowledgement

The journey of writing "The Rejoice of Celestial Odyssey" has been an incredible adventure, and it would not have been possible without the support and encouragement of many remarkable individuals.

First and foremost, I extend my deepest gratitude to my family, whose unwavering love and belief in me have been my greatest motivators. To my friends, thank you for your patience and for always being there to celebrate the milestones along the way.

I would also like to express my sincere appreciation to my parents, mentors in the field of space exploration and literature. Your insights and guidance have enriched my understanding and fueled my passion for this subject. Special thanks to my Parents and teachers, for their invaluable contributions and inspiration.

Lastly, to my readers—your curiosity and enthusiasm inspire me to share these stories.

May this odyssey ignite your own dreams of exploration and discovery.
Thank you all for being a part of this journey.

Preface

In an age where the cosmos beckons with its unfathomable mysteries and celestial wonders, "The Rejoice of Celestial Odyssey" embarks on a journey that transcends the boundaries of our world. This book is a celebration of humanity's innate desire to explore, to question, and to dream beyond the confines of our earthly existence.

As we navigate the pages of this odyssey, we will delve into the heart of space exploration—its triumphs, its challenges, and the spirit of discovery that fuels our quest for knowledge. From the earliest astronomers who gazed at the stars with wonder to the pioneers who ventured into the void, this journey pays homage to those who dared to reach for the infinite.

The Twinkling Star

In the velvet cloak of night,
A twinkling star takes flight.
With the help of it 's blaze,
in the shape of rays.

shining with a gleam,
In the way of beam .
You help us to find way home,
In our aspect you are like a stone.

You create shapes in sky,
But we couldn't reach you why.
Because you are too for away,
When we can catch you sway.

When you start to blink,
In the twilight's gentle wink.
Each moment sparkles, pure and true,
A symphony of me and you.

Night Light

Hey Moon ! you arrive at night,
And you give wonderful light.
You are so high up in sky,
We see you with our eye.

We depend on your light ,
During the night.
You have your own model,
Also you go in your own tunnel.

When the sun set you rise up,
You have your own club.
With full twinkling stars,
It's like an light of of a car.

you grace the velvet night,
You are extremely bright.
Her glow caresses the sleeping sea,
A silver whisper in the twilight's plea.

Asteroids Belt

In the silent void where shadows dance,
A wanderer drifts in a timeless trance.
Echoes of the cosmos in their flight,
Whispers of creation, dark and light.

Fragments of planets, once whole and grand,
Now scattered like seeds across the dark
strand.
Those asteroids going in a unswerving line,
All the asteroids in their own way there fine.

After some orbit of planet you are the next ,
The word asteroid is made up of 8 text.
But you are in larger scale compared to those
letter,
Actually quite or a bit better.

You are something which blows our minds,
But actually we do things like a blind.
You are a floating Rock on the space,
In a quite big place.

Ice Giant

Ho! my dear friends Uranus and Neptune,
In you, also there is something called Lipton.
Frosted oceans stretch in a glimmering hue,
backscattering the stars in deep, of endless
blue.

Hey Uranus you are the gigantic of ice,
In your cold way you are so nice.
Ice giants roam in the cold of space,
A distant orb in a tranquil embrace.

With each silent spin through the vastness of
space,
It beckons the dreamers to join in the chase.
Neptune you are another the Uranus second
face,
You have the setting of eight in the space.

Neptune frolic, distant king,
With sapphire storms that twist and sing.
His throne of ice, on an ocean of blue,
Reflects the stars, a celestial hue.

You guys consist of hydrogen and helium,
But generation of ice, you are premium.
Two distant worlds, each unique in hue,
Neptune and Uranus, a cosmic view.

The Planet Saturn

Saturn spins in regal grace,
A distant king in the celestial space.
With gale that swirl in a agile waltz,
A titan of gas, with its mystic vaults.

In the solar system you are so unique,
It is basically when I speak.
You have a ring around you,
But because of the backscattering is like blue.

billions of fractions of ice, chaff and rocks,
The word billion is a ultimate shock.
You are also the gas giant,
To study about you we should be Scient.

You are so far away from us,
Actually what is inside you is Anonymous.
A beacon of wonder, both near and far,
An anonymous jewel, a wandering star.

The Dwarf Planet

Once a planet, a title once grand,
Now a dwarf, you still take your stand.
Pluto, the wanderer, small and proud,
In icy silence, beneath a starry shroud.

Before you were like your friends,
Currently as a dwarf, it is the end.
You take orbit in a long way,
In Pluto's days ,it is 6.4 Earth days.

Hey friend, being a dwarf doesn't matter,
Like being taller or shorter .
Dwarf is also important in solar system,
If we need to research you, we need Wisdom.

Pluto spins a tale so old,
Of mysteries in darkness told.
Though charts may shift, and labels fade,
In stardust dreams, I'm unafraid.

Kuiper Belt

Beyond Neptune's frozen edge,
A realm of icy bodies pledge,
Eris glimmers, Pluto's charm,
Each body holds a cosmic balm.

A guardian of dreams long cast,
In the universe, vast and vast.
In the outer circle of all the orbits,
Bypass Neptune, Pluto way which is split.

A cradle of wonders, ancient and wise,
Where starlight fades and new worlds rise.
Like asteroid belt, you are in the largest scale,
Behind all the planet, a big rainfall of hail.

So here in my forum, with faith as my guide,
I'll chart the vast reaches, my spirit the tide,
A scientist in wonder's grip,
As I trace the cosmos on this trip.

Trojans

The Trojans stood with hearts ablaze,
In twilight's glow, they faced the frays.
Brave warriors in armor shone,
With soul of fire, they proclaimed their own.

So let us guard what we hold dear,
With wisdom sharp and vision clear.
Oh, clever minds, with schemes so grand,
They thought they'd found a master plan.

In silent wait, they bide their time,
To shift the fate with stealthy rhyme.
In binary whispers, secrets dwell,
Encoded scripts, a hidden spell.

With algorithms forged in shadowed labs,
Exploiting vulnerabilities, a web of jabs.
Molecular whispers in DNA's thread,
Carrying messages, where life is bred.

With cytoplasmic paths, they navigate,
In a microscopic world, they orchestrate.

Planet Venus

An infernal Frolic in a slow-motion blaze,
Veiled in clouds of sulfuric haze.
Greenhouse gases, a heat intense,
Atmospheric pressure, crushing, dense.

Reflecting the light of distant stars,
Surface of basalt, with craters like scars.

Unraveling mysteries of this fiery dome,
Explorers have ventured, their probes sent to roam.
The clouds of sulfur, the heat we believe,
From Venera's gaze, we learned to perceive.

In a tapestry woven from stories untold,
Stars scatter like secrets, ancient and bold.
As scientists gather, each breakthrough a toy,
In history's pages, her name whispers joy.

Unveiling the mysteries, sublime and prime,
Galileo's gaze through the lenses of time.
To the tales of explorers who dared to persist,
From Venusian landscapes, shrouded in mist.

Mother Earth

In her arms, the mountains rise,
Wrapped in clouds, beneath vast skies.
In whispered winds through ancient trees,
Her laughter dances with the leaves.

She gives us place to live,
Mother Earth in you, we survive.
We have our mother's,
For everyone your the mother who is clever.

Rivers carve their winding ways,
Reflecting sun's warm, golden rays.
Also you protect us,
Comparing to you we are less.

To keep the rivers clean,
And keep the forest green.
And are melts of pollution,
Remember there is a solution.

You also have a heart,
And it is extraordinary smart .

You are the best of all,
So you have to take more rest.

Our Star Sun

Ho! sun you are the greatest star in the space ,
You have the most of the place .
according to all the planets you are the great,
Through your vitamin d energy you are our
best mate.

You are the vital source of light,
And it is very bright .
As you dusk to set,
rays paint beautiful colours that we wont
forget.

You are the shining Star forever ,
Always your love and ever.
You are the best,
I thank you for the splendid fest.

Mars Planet

Oh Mars! Your beauty holds a spark,
In the barren lands, a glowing mark.
Mountains arise, like ancient kings,
Veins of canyons where the memory clings.

Before the life of mars,
Like earth could be see the star.
All the planets are there on force,
But you have your own source.

Rovers roam on this rust-colored land,
Unraveling secrets with a tireless hand.
With rovers rolling on rusty plains,
And telescopes tracing light's refrains.

We sketch the tales of what might be,
A tapestry of hope and mystery

The Milky Way Galaxy

In the velvet cloak of dark,
In your place you Mark.
You are like a river of milk,
If we can see you ,we try to link.

If we each do our share,
To show our galaxy you care.
Nebulae bloom like floral dreams,
In colors that shimmer, glint, and gleam.

Black holes lurking, mysteries vast,
Guardians of the shadows cast.
In the manner of post,
Your messages , we believe and trust.

In the tapestry of time, you weave us so near,
A galaxy of stories, each one crystal clear.
With each twinkling star, we're forever
entwined,
Grateful for the wonders that spark the mind.

Gas Giant

In the vast embrace of the cosmic night,
Jupiter reigns with a stormy might.
Galilean moons in a celestial waltz,
Drawn close by his gravity, a dance that
exalts.

A giant of gas, swirling with might,
A tempest of storms in the deep cosmic night.
Oh, king of the night, in your majesty's gaze,
You hold the cosmos in a cosmic embrace.

Many people come to research you,
Because your enormous planet ,that true.
You are the lord of all the planets in solar
system ,
But everyone in earth are Materialism.

You have many moons ,
You ever had a noon,
In your shadow, the cosmos sings,
Jupiter, you are the king of kings.

The Black Hole

17

In Center of galaxy, a darkness lies,
A hidden titan, where light defies.
Where escape becomes naught but a pledge,
Event horizon: the boundary's edge.

For in every black hole, a paradox thrives-—
Death and rebirth, where the universe strives.
Where light meets its end in the stillness of
air,
A swirling vortex, dark as despair.

What lies beyond in the infinite deep?
In the silence of voids, where secrets keep.
Questions of existence, the nature of law--
Mysteries linger in this cosmic maw.

Silver Star: Mercurius

A Mercury planet, carved by Rains,
In the deepness of space, where quietness take
reigns.
Erode the surface, their grip to pierce,
Eons of weather, relentless and fierce.

Atmosphere thin, with elements rare,
Mercury planet is the one of the will fare.
You consists of many components,
But do you have a opponent.

In the wide universe ,all the things are right
Mountains rise with tectonic might.
Creating mountains, valleys, and oceans wide.
Tectonic plates shift, in a slow, steady glide.

Hydrologic rhythms, a natural chain,
Water in cycles, from vapor to rain.
A Mercury planet, in the void, it's grown,
Composed of silicates, metals, and stone.

Universum Ignoratum
(Unknown Universe)

In cosmos stretches, vast and bright,
A frolic of fate divine.
Beyond what we see, in shadows concealed,
The universe whispers what science has
revealed.

What echoes of the past?
The mysteries are cast.
What secrets dwell in the cosmic sea?
In every pulse of energy,

Carrying messages from stars to our feet,
Neutrinos glide, elusive and fleet.
Why there are hidden things ?
This mysterious makes up about 27% which
brings.

Stellar nurseries cradle the young,
Hydrogen fuses, and new worlds are spun.

The Nitrogen Element

In the atmosphere, where the blue sky reigns,
Nitrogen reigns supreme, with 78% of its
chains.
A diatomic gas, N_2 in its form,
Colorless, odorless, a silent norm.

Nitrogen, silent, with no hue,
Guarding life in the morning dew.
Hey our first best guardian,
To hard to for us to hearken.

In the cold of the liquid, it's harnessed with
care,
Preserving the past, like a breath of fresh air.
In proteins and greens, your essence remains,
Fueling the growth through the sun's warm
refrains.

From the roots of the soil, to the stars up
high,
It nourishes the plants, under the colossal sky.
In the lab, you chill with a frosty embrace,
Preserving the future, in a scientific race.

So here's to nitrogen, quiet and grand,
The backbone of our living, in our planet and
strand.
So here in this poem, let science align,
With nature's own rhythm, in a cycle divine.

The Amazing Helium

In a world of elements, light and free,
A whisper of laughter, a bubble's glee.
Being a big partner of sun ,
At moment, when it runs.

In every party, it makes hearts soar,
A magical element we can't ignore.
Atomic number, a simple pair,
In quantum realms, it finds its flair.

From gas wells deep, it's drawn with care,
In balloons, it rises, light as air.
In every bubble, in every dream,
Helium flows like a silent stream.

The Oxygen For Our Breathe

In the quiet breath of dawn's embrace,
Where whispers dance in the open space.
You're the pit-a-pat of the forestland, the
sough of the sea,
A symphony written in each living tree.
From leafy greens in sunlit hues,
To deep blue depths where silence ensues.

In the lungs of flora, in the breath of man,
Photosynthesis, nature's grand plan.
Invisible thread, binding us tight,
In every dawn, you gift us light.
Unlocking the secrets that nature designed,
In labs, you inspire the curious mind.

In cellular rhythms, it fuels the spark,
ATP's chorus ignites in the dark.
Chlorophyll's canvas, sunlight's embrace,
Transforms carbon's grip into life's warm
grace.

So here's to O2, the element grand,
In the tapestry of life, a vital strand.

Carbon-di-oxide

In the dance of life, a whisper flows,
Invisible breath where the wild wind blows.
Turning CO_2 into the essence of the world,
Plants reach for sunlight, their green leaves
unfurl.

A balancing act where life does abide,
In oceans deep, it meets the tide.
We weave our own future, in this fragile tale,
From fossil fuels burned, to every exhale.

While industry churns, painting grey skies,
Volcanoes erupt, breathing ancient sighs,
To harmonize beneath the skies,
So let us learn, with open eyes.

From bustling streets to the quiet glade,
You weave through life, a thread well-laid.